Children's talks with puppet sketches

John Hardwick

Kevin
Mayhew

First published in 2001 by
KEVIN MAYHEW LTD
Buxhall
Stowmarket
Suffolk IP14 3BW

9 8 7 6 5 4 3 2 1 0

ISBN 1 84003 716 4
Catalogue No 1500417

Cover design by Jonathan Stroulger
Edited and typeset by Elisabeth Bates
Printed and bound in Great Britain

Foreword

John Hardwick is one of those unique individuals who somehow seem to have received more than their fair share of gifts! It is something I know only too well after working alongside John for a number of years. Through that time I learnt a great deal from him and so I am especially pleased that some of that experience and expertise is available through this book. John's ability to communicate creatively, his love for the Bible and his passion to reach children of all ages for Jesus, ensure that this new resource is one that will enhance the work you do to share God's good news.

Alan Charter
Head of Missions, Scripture Union

About the author

John Hardwick is a well-known creative Christian communicator. He is the author of the *Ultimate Holiday Club Guide* and has written many children's songs, including 'God's people' and 'Nobody's a nobody'. He uses simple puppets, songs, storytelling, juggling and clowning to present the good news of Jesus Christ in imaginative ways which appeal to children of all ages.

John travels widely, leading training sessions, praise parties and all-age celebrations. He works under the banners of 'Children Woldwide' and 'Counties'.

This book is dedicated to my father, Leslie Hardwick and my late mother, Ruth Hardwick, who, since long before I was born, were involved in reaching out to children through Sunday School, midweek children's club and a beach mission at Skegness. They helped me see the importance of reaching children who often have little knowledge of the Bible or of God's love for them. I also want to dedicate it to my sister Rachel Munoz Hardwick, who first taught me the guitar and got me involved in leading school assemblies. I'd especially like to thank my wife, Rachel, and daughter, Chloe, for their love and support.

Contents

Why use puppets?

Comments from puppeteers

- A visual aid you can use time after time
- A visual aid children will ask you about even when it's not in use!
- A friend for life
- Easy to use
- Appeals to all ages
- Relatively cheap
- Wonderful for introducing and illustrating themes!
- There's one out there somewhere just waiting for you! A style and a puppet to suit you!

Variety of puppets

At some stage we have all enjoyed watching puppets in action. Puppets can be simple or complex: Sooty and Sweep, Thunderbirds, the Muppets, Spitting Image, ventriloquists' dolls/puppets; there is such a variety yet all have made their mark in the entertainment world.

Attention grabbing

Just sitting in a room with a cuddly toy on your lap will make you the centre of attention! Children love to watch puppet shows. Ventriloquists are often included in variety shows. Very few art forms can capture the imagination of both adults and children in one single performance, which is why ventriloquists often do well in talent shows.

A friend for life

Unlike many tricks or visual aids you can use your puppet time after time. It becomes a real friend to the children – someone they can relate to. When I'm out and about children often come up to me wanting to see Micky (my monkey puppet) and asking where he is and what he's up to. He's even been on the front page of newspapers, has opened school halls and been asked to cut the ribbon! I've had heads of schools asking if Micky could go and take their school assembly!

A solo performer becomes a double act

There are occasions when people have to present a children's talk or lesson on their own, for example a church minister or speaker, a Sunday school teacher or a schoolteacher. This can be limiting when it comes to trying to put across a message in a creative way time after time.

A puppet is like having an acting partner, someone to perform sketches with and bounce lines off. Another personality or character, with the advantage that they are able to practise when it suits you, without having to find a time to suit two diaries!

Puppets can be very childlike or innocent, getting into all kinds of situations. They can get away with things that a human speaker cannot! For example, Micky (my monkey puppet) often starts a sketch by going to have a closer look at the audience and then announces that he feels very much at home amongst so many monkeys!

More than just entertainment

Puppets are wonderful teaching aids. Children seem to relate easily to puppets, often being more prepared to listen to a puppet rather than a human. Puppets often get things wrong and mess up or say the wrong thing! They may not understand something, and get confused and upset. By explaining something to the puppet you're reaching your audience in an indirect but non-threatening way. The children don't feel 'got at' but get the message loud and clear!

Puppets can introduce, illustrate, or reinforce themes.

Puppets are ideal for

- children's/all-age talks in church services
- primary school assemblies
- Sunday school or midweek children's programmes
- open air gatherings.

(I often use my puppet with older people too. He's well known at several old people's homes and ladies' classes.)

Writing a script

When people first handle a puppet they normally just look around at people or start to batter them with it, without having a definite plan or idea!

However, coming up with a script is relatively easy. With a little time, practice, and imagination you'll be amazed by what you can produce.

Who are your audience?

If the majority of your audience are children, try to think through what a child's daily routine might be like. Generalise a little! Older children may like to stay in bed, while younger ones often wake the house up. Girls may spend ages brushing their hair, boys don't bother! (Or is it the other way round?) What might they have for breakfast? What are their likes and dislikes; their favourite or least favourite food, game, television programme, subject at school, pop star/group, football team, etc.?

All of these areas could be used in a puppet sketch. It will hold the children's attention because they'll want to know what the puppet's favourite is, and because you have included things which mean a lot to them.

Use everyday situations

Think of things from your childhood which made you happy or upset you. For example:
- being the person who isn't picked for a team
- being the smallest person
- your first day at school
- how you felt when someone broke something you made
- being chosen for something
- winning a competition.

Current events

Think of things you may be doing now! When I was decorating a room at home I thought to myself, 'What would a room look like if it had been decorated by my puppet?'

Keep it down to earth

The puppet is *not* the vicar, minister, preacher or worship leader.

It's not advisable for them to pray, preach the sermon, give their testimony, baptise, or take funeral services!

However, they could interview people (although some of the more serious spiritual questions could be asked by another interviewer). They could give out the weekly notices but not the serious ones.

A fast-moving visual aid

Their main strength is illustrating, introducing or reinforcing a point or theme.

Using Bible stories

Do not come up with a puppet sketch and then try to make a Bible story fit your theme. You must work the other way round, keeping true to the word of God. Choose a Bible story or passage first and then come up with a sketch to help illustrate its teaching.

Using cuddly toys or wooden spoons with faces

You may have simple props such as cuddly toys or even wooden spoons. You could put up a screen and use the puppets to act out the story as a narrator tells or reads it. You could have different people with different voices for each of the cuddly toys/spoons, etc.

Using fables and other stories

Many children's stories and fables bring out good morals. You can easily adapt these for puppet sketches.

Using backing music and backing vocals

Puppets miming along to songs can be very effective and also very funny. For example, a tiny mouse puppet singing opera (this will grab people's attention); puppets performing raps – include the cool shades; a team of puppets singing and swaying to a gospel song. You can even get tapes with puppets in dialogue so all you have to do is mime along! (If pop stars can get away with it, then why not puppets?)

Endless variety and styles!

There really is 'something for everyone' when it comes to puppets, so go on, give them a go!

Puppet to human

The whispering puppet

This is a dialogue between the puppet and the operator. The puppet pretends to talk to the operator (e.g. whispers in the operator's ear). This is relatively simple yet very effective, especially if you are a solo worker, because you have another character to bounce lines off and to do sketches with.

You are not stuck behind a puppet theatre or screen so it's easy to have good interaction with your audience. In fact you can go right up to them and even pick out an individual (e.g. if someone sneezes in the audience it's easy for the puppet to look directly at that person and say 'bless you!' – this always gets a laugh).

You don't have to cart round a theatre or screen, just a simple bag, box, basket, small dustbin or case! It's amazing how excited the children become when they recognise the bag. Therefore, be careful in the way you handle it, it's carrying a precious cargo!

Getting started

The sketch starts as soon as you pick up the bag. I often say something like: 'I've brought along a friend of mine.' While I'm saying this I pick up the bag, undo the zip a little way, and start to put my hand inside the puppet while it's still in the bag. It's important to have the puppet the right way round in the bag so that the bottom of the puppet is close to where the bag starts to open. (If the puppet is in a box then have a hole at one end of the box so that your arm goes through the hole straight into the puppet!)

When your arm is right inside the puppet and able to operate the mouth, open the rest of the zip and let the puppet peep out and look at the audience. Encourage the puppet to come right out: 'Come on, Micky, they're waiting for you.' The mood that the puppet is in determines the speed he comes out of the bag. I normally put my other hand under the puppet as though it's taking the weight; it helps to hide the fact that your other hand is inside the puppet. And now you are ready to proceed with the sketch!

Whispering techniques

As the puppet whispers in your ear, relay what the puppet is saying to the audience. At other times let the puppet whisper and just nod, keeping the audience in suspense! You and the puppet may choose to look at someone and pretend to have a private conversation, both looking at the person then at each other and shaking your heads, or laughing. The audience are longing to know what you are saying.

You can also have the puppet whisper a long sentence into your ear and then you relay a very short sentence. This always gets a laugh!

Because you are translating what the puppet is saying, you will have to adapt the wording of the scripts in places! For example, if in the script the puppet says 'I want to go for a walk,' as the puppet whispers in your ear, you will say, 'You want to go for a walk?' changing 'I' to 'You'. You'll soon get the hang of it!

Character

Give your puppet a character. It may be cheeky, a comedian, eager to learn or a bit of a 'know it all'; shy or extrovert, sporty or lazy, agrees with everything you say or argumentative!

The character may be shaped by what the puppet is or looks like. For example, a monkey puppet, like monkeys, will be generally cheeky and full of excitement.

Movement

Remember that the puppet must come across as being alive. When I first take Micky out of his bag he has a look around to see where he is. Something may catch his eye so when I'm trying to talk to him he's not taking a bit of notice! He may then start to chat about what he has seen while I try to get him to listen to me.

He will react if there is a background noise or a sudden movement nearby – he may shake with fear and hide his face in my shoulder as I comfort him and ensure him it's quite safe.

Sometimes we fall out and every time I look at him he looks away. Then, I look away when he looks at me; then as soon I as look at him again he looks away!

When he's happy his movement is quick and excitable. He even jigs around – he calls it dancing! When he's sad his movement is slow and solemn.

Facial expression

Some puppets have soft faces which means your are able to pull faces. A puppet pulling a face always gets a reaction.

Practise

Practise in front of a mirror as this helps you see what works and what doesn't. Practise the sketches, movement, whispering technique, the way you react to the puppet and pulling faces.

Sketches

With this style of puppet don't worry about knowing the sketch off by heart. After all, only you will know if you don't get it word perfect! Read the sketch over and over again. Try and remember the main points and the good jokes. Then you will have fun and be flexible enough to react to the audience.

The secret is to read it over and over again until it really sinks in and then you'll find the sketch will flow!

The end

Don't finish a sketch with you and the puppet falling out. The children may choose to side with the puppet! If the puppet has done something wrong then the sketch normally ends with the puppet going off to put it right, finishing on a positive rather than a negative note.

The puppet will then say goodbye and disappear into its bag. Never leave a puppet outside the bag and in full view, it will have no life and will ruin what you have just done and may upset some children.

After the sketch

Children or adults may ask if they can have a go with your puppet. I always say 'no' because the puppet's character will not be the same, once again ruining what you have just done.

You may choose to get the puppet out to show them again, otherwise just say that the puppet is asleep or can become grumpy when disturbed, or is just too busy!

You can do it!

I believe that with a little practice anyone can learn to use a puppet in this way. Go for it and you'll have a wonderful visual aid and a friend for life!

Puppet to puppet

A dialogue between the puppets

There are several different ways that the puppets can communicate with the audience.

- Puppets can be chatting to each other, with the operator(s) being hidden behind a black cloth in a puppet theatre or behind a screen. Puppets in dialogue with each other will require plenty of practice. If there are two or more operators then you need to know your script (otherwise you will talk over the top of each other).
- A single operator can work both puppets in a puppet theatre. This also requires plenty of practice! Have a different puppet on each arm with each having its own voice and personality. Make sure that you don't get the two mixed up! This style may sound too difficult but I know several people who have picked this up relatively quickly.

Operating the puppets

Position of the puppets

It is important for the puppets to look as though they are real and alive, therefore the position of the puppets is very important!

- Make sure the puppets are upright and not leaning to one side.
- Make sure the puppets are looking where they're meant to be looking. If the puppets are having a conversation with the audience they should look at the audience and not above their heads or at their feet. This will take practice so ask someone to watch to help you get it right.
- Do move the puppets. Turn their heads to look at each other. If they are excited then jig them around. If they are sad their movements are slower and they will look down.

Mouth movement

When we talk we start with the mouth closed and then open and close it for the different syllables and words. However, when people first try to make a puppet talk, they start with the mouth open and then close and open it for each word – the wrong way round!

- Start with the mouth closed then push the mouth open and close it again to form the different words.
- Try to keep the puppet's top lip fairly still by mainly moving your thumb (in the lower part of the mouth) to create the words.
- Don't concentrate so hard on the script that you forget to move the mouth when talking. This looks rather odd!
- When using two puppets, make sure you use the right voice with the right puppet.

The voice

Try to develop a voice for the puppet which is different from your own. It may be pitched high or low depending on the gender or age of the puppet character. You could try an accent, e.g. a country accent, Scottish, Welsh, Irish, Cockney, French, American, or a posh English accent, etc.

The character

Choose a name and a character style to suit each puppet and stick to it, e.g. quiet and shy, confident and an extrovert, intelligent, a bit of a lad, bossy, mean, crazy, cheeky.

Think about the age of each puppet, e.g. a child, teenager, adult, old person.

- What sort of voice would they have?
- What is important to them and what would their conversation be about?
- Where do they go and what do they do during the day?
- Would they listen to Radio 1, Radio 4, Classic FM or none of them?
- Would they watch TV soaps, the news, children's TV, sport, documentaries?

Do's and don'ts

- **Do** practise! You could practise in front of the mirror.
- **Don't** try to stay up too long with the puppets because your arms will tire very quickly.
- **Do** know what you are going to say, the outline and the point of the sketch.
- **Don't** forget to move the mouth when you talk, and don't use the wrong voice for the puppet. Speak clearly.
- **Do** look in the right direction and not at the ceiling or down at the floor.
- **Don't** show a dead puppet (a puppet left out for all to see).
- **Do** use humour.
- **Don't** be put off when it doesn't go quite as well as you hoped.
- **Do** have a go and have fun!

The puppet theatre

The puppet theatre is an ideal way for the operator(s) to be hidden from the audience while still being able to see a little of them to facilitate interaction. It also means that the operator's arms are bent and tucked into the body giving some support. However, the puppet theatre can be difficult to transport from place to place and space inside is limited.

A puppet screen

A puppet screen can either be a frame with a cloth covering or a more solid piece of hardboard fixed to a frame. Screens can be as large or small as you require, often depending on the size of your car.

You can paint all kinds of designs on these. A hardboard screen is easy to cut and therefore can be turned into a wonderful set such as a castle or a ship, or let your imagination run wild – very visual, attracting attention!

You can have several operators behind one screen. However, as the operators normally have their arms outstretched above their heads, this becomes tiring after a short while. It's also very difficult to have interaction with the audience. The staging and number of puppets can work out quite expensive, but remember you can use puppets over and over again. You can use these in church services and in schools and they are a wonderful attraction in the open air.

A team of puppeteers can come up with some wonderful ideas and may become close friends!

Music

All the songs quoted in the sketches on the following pages are from *34 Songs for All Occasions* (see page 80 for full details).

Actions speak louder than words

Theme: Father's Day

Aim

To show that it's no good to say you'll do something and then forget, or it's no good to say you love someone if you always let them down. You need to prove it by your actions.

Song

VIP *or*
Think about such things

Puppet sketch

John   *(to audience)* Yesterday Micky was my hero!

Micky   *(looking very pleased with himself)* Thanks!

John   I was in a hurry to go out and the washing was still on the line. 'Leave that, I'll get it in for you,' said Micky. There was a programme on TV I wanted to see. 'I'll set the video for you,' said Micky. *(Micky nods)* I needed to get some milk from the shop for this morning's breakfast. 'I'll fetch that for you,' said Micky. *(he is still nodding)* There was some washing-up in the sink. 'Leave the washing-up! Just go! I'll do it!' I was very pleased with Micky for volunteering to do all these things for me.

Micky   Oh dear!

John   Yes, 'oh dear' indeed. This morning Micky is not my hero! *(Micky looks away and refuses to look John in the eye)* The washing is still on the line and it rained last night! *(Micky looks guilty)* The washing-up is still in the sink, which means no clean dishes for breakfast! But that doesn't really matter, seeing he didn't get any milk anyway! He didn't set the video recorder, so I can't see the TV programme that I wanted to watch!

Micky   *(looking around)* Nice room this, isn't it?

John   Stop trying to change the subject! Actions speak louder than words! I was relying on you and you let me down!

Micky   I'm really sorry. Honestly.

John I know you are. I'm not that angry really, Micky, but if you say you're going to do something then make sure that you do. Keep the promise because actions speak louder than words!

Bible story

The parable of the two sons
Matthew 21:28-31

A father had two sons. He went to the eldest son and said, 'Son, will you go and work in the vineyard today?'

'Oh Dad, I can't today. I've got so much to do!'

So the father asked the other son the same thing. 'Of course I will, Dad.'

Meanwhile, the eldest son felt guilty. 'My father does so much for me; I ought to go and do some work in the vineyard.' So off he went.

However, the other son completely forgot about what he had promised to do and went off and did his own thing!

Which one did as his father had asked?

Actions speak louder than words!

Round-up

If you promise to be somewhere, be there! If you promise to do something, do it! If you say you love someone, prove it and treat them right! Your actions speak louder than words.

Prayer

Lord, I pray that we won't be all mouth and no actions, and if we say we'll do something that we will keep our word. Amen.

A huge thank-you!

Aim

To encourage children not to take things or what people do for them for granted, and to show that saying thank you can make a huge difference.

Song

A huge thank-you!

Puppet sketch

John   Hey, Ralph, it's been ages since I saw you. *(Ralph is a dog puppet)* I was just going past a shop and saw something I thought you might like. So here, this is for you. *(John gives Ralph a gift)*

Ralph   Great! *(starts to open it)*

John   I think you've forgotten something! *(Ralph ignores him, he's interested in his gift)* Two little words?

Ralph   *(finally getting into the gift)* Oh, blow!

John   No, those are not the words I meant!

Ralph   *(looks fed up)* That's not what I wanted! Oh, blow! Can't you get anything right?

John   Well, I'm sorry *(sarcastically)*. I didn't have to get you anything!

Ralph   The ball's all right! It's just not what I wanted! I wanted a doggy joke book. *(Vary your gift to suit your puppet; my gift to Ralph is a very cool-looking ball to play with.)*

John   *(now getting very annoyed)* OK! I'll have it back and give it to a dog who would love to have such a gift!

Ralph   You can't do that!

John   I can! There were lots of people in the shop and I had to wait for ages, but I thought that it would be worth it, just to watch you open the gift and see your face light up! But instead you just said 'Oh, blow,' and sulked. You didn't even bother to say thank you!

Ralph   Gosh, I've upset you, haven't I? Sorry I was a grump. It's actually a very cool ball and we could have a lot of fun with it! I could throw it and you could fetch it, or the other way round . . . if you like. If the offer's still there then I would love it!

John   Of course it is!

Ralph   G-R-E-A-T! Thanks, it's ace! *(licks John's face then throws the ball)* Fetch!

John   Oi! Cheek! You fetch – you're the dog! *(to the audience)* It's amazing how the atmosphere changes when someone is really thankful for something! Ralph wants to go now and play with his ball. Let's give him a round of applause!

Bible story

The ten lepers
Luke 17:11-19

There were ten men in the story and I reckon they were in a hurry, a hurry to get home. They wouldn't have been allowed home for a long time; it may have been years and they probably thought that they would never be able to go home again. But now they were on their way to their homes!

I wonder what sort of things they may have been excited about. One may have said, 'Just think, tonight I'll have a *home-cooked* meal. I can't wait!' Another may have said, 'I'll see the children again! I bet they have really grown. I can't wait!' Another may have said, 'I'll be able to kiss the wife – I can't wait!' They must all have been so excited!

But why hadn't they been allowed home? They hadn't done anything wrong and been in prison; they hadn't been in the army, or working away from home.

They had all caught the dreaded skin disease, probably leprosy, which meant that their skin would turn white and start to flake off. They would gradually get weaker and weaker and would eventually die. They would have to leave their homes and families because they didn't want them to catch it. Also they would have to live outside the village. It must have been a very sad time for everyone.

But then one day, these ten men heard Jesus was in town. They would have heard about him, about his kindness and great power, a man of God. So they stood at a distance and shouted, 'Jesus! Master! Take pity on us!' Jesus did and he healed them! Then he told them to show themselves to the priests who would confirm that they were indeed better. This meant that they were allowed to go home. They would have been so happy and they would have rushed home.

But one of them, a Samaritan, suddenly remembered how Jesus had healed him and changed his life for the better. So he went to find him and fell at Jesus' feet, thanking him and praising him for all he had done. Jesus said, 'There were ten men who were healed. Where are the other nine? Why is it only one has come back to praise God?' Jesus said to him, 'Get up and go; your faith has made you well.'

One said 'thank you', nine didn't bother!

Round-up

People do things for us every day (list a few). How often do we thank them? It can make a huge difference and put a smile on their faces.

Prayer

Thank you God for all the things you do and provide for us. Help us to remember to say thank you to you and to all those people who give up their time to help us. Amen.

Be a good host

Aim

To show how important it is to make people feel welcome, to include them, look after them and provide for them.

Song

Image of God

Puppet sketch

John   Hey Micky! I saw your mate Tango the other day. *(to audience)* Tango is an orang-utan.

Micky   He's got long hair!

John   Micky often goes to Tango's house to play after school.

Micky   We eat bananas and have a banana milkshake, then we go and climb the tree in his garden. After that we go in the house and have ice cream! – banana flavour – then we play games – it's great!

John   Tango went to your house the other day, didn't he? But when I saw him he was very upset. What happened? Did you argue?

Micky   *(looking guilty)* No.

John   Come on, Micky. What did you do?

Micky   Nothing!

John   Come on, you must have done something to upset him! What did you do?

Micky   Nothing!

John   Yes, that's true! Tango's mum told me you did nothing for him! When he came round, did you give him a drink? *(Micky looks guilty)* No, I didn't think so. Did you give him a banana?

Micky   There was only one left!

John   So you ate it yourself! Did you play any games?

Micky   Sort of.

John   Yes, I heard. You bet him that he couldn't do the washing-up as quick as you could. You tricked him into doing the washing-up for you while you went upstairs and played your games! Oh, Micky! What sort of friend, or host are you? Leaving him like that! If you ask someone round to your house you have to look after them the same way Tango looked after you.

Micky   I'm going to invite him again, but this time I'm going to really look after him and give him a great time!

John   Good! *(to audience)* Let's say goodbye to Micky and let him plan what he intends to do next time Tango goes round. *(puts Micky into his bag)*

Bible story

Luke 7:36-50

There is a story a bit like this in the Bible. In Bible days there were no cars. Everyone had to walk. It was hot and roads were dusty, which meant that your feet got filthy-dirty, hot, sweaty and smelly! So if you were invited to someone's house, your host would wash your feet, welcome you with a kiss and give you some olive oil for your head to help you cool down.

A man called Simon the Pharisee invited Jesus to his house, but Simon didn't wash Jesus' feet, or welcome him with a kiss, or give him any olive oil for his head. He just showed him to his place and Jesus sat down.

Jesus must have felt very uncomfortable. He still had hot, sweaty feet and no olive oil to cool him down. He hadn't been properly welcomed!

Suddenly a woman burst through the door. She went straight up to Jesus and started to cry and her tears fell on his feet. We don't know much about this woman, maybe she had been healed by Jesus, or maybe Jesus had been kind to her in some way. We do know that she was very grateful to Jesus.

Her tears washed Jesus' feet which she dried with her hair. She then broke open a jar of perfume and covered his feet with it. She then kissed his feet. Simon, the host, thought that this was horrible! 'Yuck! Fancy Jesus allowing her to do that to him!'

Jesus said to him, 'Simon, I came to your house. You gave me no water to wash my feet, but she washed my feet with her tears and dried them with her hair. You did not welcome me with a kiss, or provide me with olive oil, but she has covered my feet with perfume.'

(Ask the children) Who really welcomed Jesus and looked after him? Was it the host Simon, or the woman?

The woman was the one who really welcomed Jesus.

Round-up

If we have someone come to our house, or someone new come to school, let's go out of our way to make them feel welcome, provide for them, and look after them.

Prayer

Lord, thank you for all the people we know and all the new people we meet. We pray that we will always make people welcome. Amen.

Better to give than to receive

Theme: Harvest Festival

Aim

It is often very difficult to give something away that is important to us, but often other people may be in desperate need of that particular thing. It is better to give than to receive.

Song

Variety, variety

Puppet sketch

Micky   I love this time of year! Look at all the different types of fruit. I like fruit!

John   Yes, we know you do. Isn't it great to see so much variety? Different types of fruit, different types of trees, different types of birds and animals, lots of colours and shades. God made so much variety.

Micky   I love harvest time!

John   I know you do. *(to audience)* At our church we have a Harvest Festival and Micky took a basket of food to an old lady in the church who needs help when it comes to shopping. *(to Micky)* Do you remember taking it to her?

Micky   Of course! She's a very friendly lady.

John   She said you were a very polite young man, but then she said: 'He does like his fruit, doesn't he?' What did she mean by that?

Micky   While we sat around, chatting, one of the grapes caught my eye. She noticed me looking at it and so she offered me a grape.

John   Of course you said 'No', didn't you? Because you knew those grapes were for her. *(Micky looks around trying to ignore the question)* Micky, you didn't have one, did you?

Micky   Yes, I'm afraid so, and one grape led to another . . .

John   More! How many did you have?

Micky   All of them. That's when I saw it.

John   Saw what?

Micky   A juicy peach looking at me.

John   Micky, you didn't have that too, did you? *(Micky looks very guilty)* Oh, Micky! How could you! The church collected that food for the lady, not for you! You can get fruit for yourself whenever you like.

Micky   But I like fruit!

John   I know, but it was for her. Did you have any more?

Micky   Er . . . yes, an apple, an orange and a banana.

John   Did you leave her any fruit at all?

Micky   Yes! Of course! A lemon. I don't like lemons.

John   Oh, Micky! I think you ought to write a letter saying that you're sorry for eating all her fruit.

Micky   Good idea. Bye!

Bible story

Jesus feeds the five thousand
John 8

It is hard to give away the things we like, but sometimes it's really good when we do. Like the boy who gave away his precious lunch.

One day a huge crowd of people followed Jesus. They wanted to hear him speak – they probably hoped he would perform a miracle. The crowd stayed there for many hours listening to Jesus.

Jesus realised that these people were getting hungry and needed some food. So he said to one of his friends, 'They need some food. Feed them.'

'I can't do that!' answered his friend. 'Where on earth can we get enough food to feed all these people?'

There were at least five thousand men plus women and children!

A small boy overheard. He had some food – his lunch, five small loaves of bread and two small fish. He would have been hungry himself, but he looked around at the hungry crowd and chose to give it all to Jesus. He knew Jesus was someone very special. 'He will know what to do,' he thought to himself.

Jesus gladly accepted the gift and broke the food. The food kept coming and coming, and coming, and coming. Jesus' friends took food to the people at the back of the crowd, and to the people at the sides and finally the people at the front, including the little boy!

Round-up

Everyone had plenty to eat, all because that little boy was prepared to give away something very important to him – his lunch! It's often better to give than to receive.

Prayer

Lord, thank you for the harvest, but we know that some countries do not have as good harvests as we do. We pray that we shall share what we have and be fair to others. Amen.

Christmas means . . .

Aim

To show that Christmas is not just toys and Father Christmas, but that it is when Christians celebrate the time that God came to the world he created.

Song

A band of angels

Puppet sketch

Micky   Guess what!

John   What?

Micky   It's nearly Christmas and you know what Christmas means, don't you? Presents! *(Micky bounces around full of excitement)*

John   Yes, Micky, but you know Christmas means more than just presents, don't you?

Micky   Of course! Christmas means Father Christmas and you know what he brings – presents!

John   Well, yes, but Christmas means more than Father Christmas and presents.

Micky   I know. Christmas means parties and guess what you get at parties – PRESENTS !

John   Oh, Micky! Christmas means more than parties, Father Christmas and presents.

Micky   I know. Christmas means trees – and what do you find at the bottom of most Christmas trees? PRESENTS!

John   Oh, Micky!

Micky   I know what else Christmas means!

John   You do?

Micky   Aunties and uncles – and guess what they bring.
P – R – E – S – E – N – T – S !

John   Micky, read this *(he hands him a Bible open at Luke 2)*. It will tell you about a very special baby. He's what Christmas is all about!

Micky   Excellent! *(Micky excitedly dashes into the bag with the Bible)*

John   I wonder how well you know the Christmas story. I'm going to tell you the story, but I'm going to put in a few mistakes. See if you can spot them and at the end we'll put them right.

Bible story

Luke 2:4-14

Once upon a time there was a grand knight. His name was Sir Joseph. He was a brave, handsome man who rode a white stallion, a fine horse! He was madly in love with a beautiful young lady. Her name was Princess Mary. They decided to marry and not long after she gave birth to a boy. They named him Jesus.

They went to the palace and placed him in a golden cot. Many kings, queens and important lords and ladies came to celebrate his birth. The town crier went into the streets to announce the birth of the new king. They all lived happily ever after. The end.

Did you spot any mistakes? There were quite a few of them.

First of all, it's not a fairy story, it's a true story.

Joseph wasn't a brave knight on a white horse. What was he and what did he have to ride? He was a carpenter and he rode a donkey.

Was Mary a princess? No, she was just a normal young girl.

Jesus was a special baby, but was he born in a palace and did he have a golden cot? No, when he was born, he was put in a manger because there was no room for them in the inn.

There were no lords and ladies, but there were visitors. Who were they? Shepherds and wise men.

There wasn't a town crier, but who did announce the birth of Jesus to the shepherds? . . . A band of angels!

Sing: A band of angels

Round-up

If Jesus had been born in a palace the shepherds wouldn't have been allowed in, but Jesus was born in a place where all could go and see. Christmas is for everyone – everyone is welcome to celebrate the birth of Jesus.

Prayer

Father God, thank you for this special time of year. Help us to remember what Christmas really means! Amen.

Dare to be different

Aim

To show that you don't have to follow the crowd when you know they are doing something wrong.

Song

Image of God

Puppet sketch

John   Micky, what are you doing tonight?

Micky   Why? What do you know?

John   Pardon? I only asked you what you were doing tonight! What do you mean, what do I know?

Micky   Has anyone been talking?

John   Talking about what?

Micky   Em, nice weather!

John   OK, Micky, what are you up to?

Micky   Nothing! So no one has mentioned the apples then?

John   Only you!

Micky   Apples, did I mention apples?

John   Yes, you jolly well did, so what is going on?

Micky   Some friends and I are going to get some apples tonight, that's all!

John   What, from the greengrocer's?

Micky   No.

John   Supermarket?

Micky   No.

John   Where, then?

Micky   From Mr Jones.

John   That's nice of him – to give you some apples.

Micky   He's not giving them to us!

John   You're buying some apples from him!

Micky   Not exactly. He's got thousands of apples so we thought we would pick some!

John   That's kind of you, to pick apples for him.

Micky   They aren't for him!

John   Who are they for then?

Micky   Us, of course. He's got thousands and we only want one or two!

John   WHAT! That's stealing!

Micky   Is it? My mates said that we're doing Mr Jones a favour by getting rid of some of them for him.

John   Your mates are wrong! It's stealing, so don't do it!

Micky   If I don't go they'll call me a chicken!

John   Then they are blind. You're a monkey, not a chicken!

Micky   But, but, but!

John   No buts, it's wrong and you know it. Why don't you and your mates go and see Mr Jones and offer to pick his apples for him? I'll come with you if you like. He would probably appreciate a hand and he may give you some as a reward!

Micky   What a brill idea! I'll go and tell my mates! Bye!

Bible story

Twelve spies
Numbers 13

God had promised his people a brand-new land! A land flowing with milk and honey!

His people were living in the desert. It was hot, there was no grass, not many trees and no shade, so they were very excited about going into the new land. Moses, their great leader, chose twelve men who would cross the River Jordan to spy out the land. 'See what the people are like who live there. What is the land like? Is it fertile, good for growing things?' he said.

It must have been very exciting, spying out the land, and after forty days they returned to Moses and the people.

They were carrying a huge bunch of grapes! 'The land's great!' shouted two of the spies. 'Let's go today.' But the other ten spies disagreed.

'No!' they shouted. 'The land is useless and the people who live there are big and strong. They will destroy us.'

But the land wasn't useless, it was good land, you just had to look at the grapes to see that. These were God's people, they had God on their side; they didn't have to be afraid of anyone!

However, the people chose to listen to the ten spies who were wrong, rather than the two spies who were right. They ended up living in the desert rather than enjoying God's promised land.

Round-up

It's better to do what is right rather than follow the crowd if the crowd is wrong! Dare to be different!

Prayer

Father God, help us to be brave and choose to do what is right, even if everyone else chooses to do what is wrong! Amen.

Don't be in such a hurry

Theme: Listening

Aim

To show how important it is to listen to people who know what they are doing. Often people are in too much of a hurry to listen properly and then wonder why it all goes wrong!

Song

Think about things *or*
Trust in the Lord

Puppet sketch

John   *(explaining to children)* I've been decorating at home!

Micky   And me!

John   *(in a hesitant voice)* Yes, Micky has been helping.

Micky   Not only helping. I've done a whole room on my own in record time.

John   No, you have not!

Micky   Yes, I have! You know, when you went shopping last night, I decided I would paper the spare bedroom.

John   *(looking very worried)* You didn't!

Micky   Yes! In record time.

John   Have you made a good job of it?

Micky   Of course! You have shown me how to do it enough times!

(phone rings)

John   *(pretending to talk to someone at home on the phone)* Hi! What do you mean, 'What have I done to the spare room?' It looks like it's been decorated by a monkey? It's a right mess and it's all lumpy? It wasn't me, it was Micky! Yes, bye!

Micky   Were they impressed by my speed?

John	*(trying to be calm)* Micky, why did you paper over the top of the old paper?
Micky	To save time.
John	But there were holes in the plaster that needed filling and some of the old paper had torn off! And where are the light switches and sockets?
Micky	It's quicker to go over the top.
John	Need I ask what happened to the windows and even *the door*?
Micky	You're angry, aren't you?
John	Yes! Why didn't you listen to me when I told you how to do it?
Micky	I did!
John	Then why didn't you do it the way I showed you?
Micky	Because I thought you were just being fussy!
John	Micky, how many rooms have you decorated?
Micky:	None. Well, one, now.
John	I've decorated lots of rooms, I've learnt from experience!
Micky	I thought I would impress you if I did it quickly.
John	If you had listened in the first place, this would never have happened. If someone is teaching you something, you have to listen carefully, and follow the instructions. That way you'll get it right. Don't be in such a hurry!
Micky	I want to go now. I want to try and think of a way I can make it up to everyone.

Bible story

The wise and foolish builders
Luke 6:46-49

Jesus was a very clever man. Everyone was amazed at the things he could do. He performed miracles, his teaching was very interesting and many people thought that he was a great man of God.

One day he told this story. There were two men who each decided to build himself a house. The first man started to dig down deep and laid the foundation upon rock. The other man couldn't be bothered with all that. 'Looks like hard work to me. And anyway, it's going to rain soon!' he said to himself. So he didn't bother digging a foundation down to the rock. He built his house on sandy ground. He would finish his house a long time before the other man.

Sure enough, it did start to rain. The second man could probably see the first man still working on his house. He probably laughed to himself. Finally the first man finished his house.

The rain poured and poured. The nearby river overflowed and the wind blew hard against the houses. Both men would have been very pleased that they had finished their houses. Both men would have watched the water getting higher and higher (gulp). But the first man who dug down to the rock didn't need to worry. His house had a firm foundation. However, the other man did need to worry. Cracks appeared. The cracks became holes. The water poured in. He tried to mop it up and block the holes, but the water kept coming! The holes got bigger and bigger, and the walls started to collapse into the water. The whole house, along with the man inside it, was swept away. If only he had spent a little extra time digging a foundation, this would not have happened.

Jesus said, 'Those who hear my words and obey them are like the wise man who built his house upon the rock, those who hear my words and ignore them are like the foolish man.'

Round-up

The foolish man and Micky were both in too much of a hurry and didn't follow instructions. It's important not only to listen to people who know best, but also to follow their instructions.

Prayer

Lord, thank you for people who teach us so many good things. I pray that we will not only listen, but also follow their instructions. Thank you for the Bible which is full of good advice. I pray that we will read it and follow its instructions. Amen.

Forgiving isn't easy

Aim

To show that we all make mistakes and let each other down. Sometimes it is hard to forgive those who have wronged us, but we must try otherwise bitterness and hatred will take over.

Song

One or two words or
VIP

Puppet sketch

John   *(to audience)* Micky was going to the circus last night with his mates. I wonder how he got on. *(to Micky)* So, Micky, was it good?

Micky   Apparently, yes.

John   Excellent! Were there clowns?

Micky   Apparently, yes.

John   Flying trapeze?

Micky   Apparently, yes.

John   Tightrope walkers?

Micky   Apparently, yes.

John   A candyfloss store?

Micky   Apparently, yes.

John   So it was great?

Micky   Apparently, yes.

John   Micky, why do you keep saying 'apparently'?

Micky   Because my best mates were meant to pick me up, but they forgot me!

John   Oh, no! So you didn't go! Then how do you know it was such a great time?

Micky   Because right at the very end they remembered me and came round to apologise, and told me what a great time they had had!

John   Oh, Micky! Maybe you can go another night.

Micky   No, it was the circus' last performance in our town. I've missed out. But don't worry, I've planned how I will get my own back!

John   I don't like the sound of that. What are you planning to do?

Micky   I'm having a mega party. There will be clowns, flying trapeze, tightrope walkers, a candyfloss store, and everyone is invited.

John   Great!

Micky   Apart from my so-called friends.

John   Hang-on, Micky! We all need friends, and friends are bound to let us down from time to time. If you're not careful, you'll have no friends to climb trees with, or play football with, or lots of things. If you invite them they will be so surprised and they will know that you are a really great guy.

Micky   But it's so hard. They left me out.

John   Forgiving is always hard, but remember we all let people down. How would you feel if someone refused to forgive you.

Micky   OK, I'll invite them. Now excuse me, I have a party to organise!

Bible story

The unforgiving servant
Matthew 18:23-35

Jesus told a story about a king. This king was very, very rich, and he was good and generous.

One day he was doing his accounts when he noticed that one of his servants owed him millions of pounds. So he ordered the man to come to see him.

'You owe me a great deal of money!'

'I know,' said the servant.

'Well, when are you going to pay it back?' asked the king.

'I'm not . . . well actually, I can't. It's just too much!' said the servant.

'You know what I'll be forced to do – I'll have to sell you and your family as slaves,' said the king.

'Oh, no! Please, please, please – pretty please – don't!' begged the servant. 'I will pay it back somehow, but please don't sell us as slaves. Be patient with me, please!'

The king felt sorry for him. 'I know what I'll do,' said the king. 'I'll let you off the whole amount. Now go and don't get into debt again!'

The servant was amazed and so happy as he left.

Then he met a fellow servant who owed him a few pounds. 'Pay-up,' he demanded, 'or I'll throw you in jail!'

His fellow servant fell on his knees and pleaded with him, 'Be patient with me and I will pay you back!'

But the first servant refused and had him thrown in jail.

The news of what the first servant had done reached the king. So he called him in.

'You worthless slave!' he said. 'I let you off the whole amount that you owed me, but you refused to show mercy to your fellow servant!'

So he had the servant flung in jail!

Round-up

We need to be like the king, willing to forgive, and not like the servant who refused to forgive.

Prayer

Father God, help us to realise that we all make mistakes, and although it may be hard, help us to forgive one another. Amen.

If I were a king!

Theme: Palm Sunday

Aim

To show what good leaders should be like. Christians believe that Jesus is king, but he is very different to other kings.

Song

Come on, let's celebrate *or*
Sing hosanna, shout hooray

Puppet sketch

(Micky is asleep in his bag, so everyone calls for him. Micky wakes up not knowing where he is.)

Micky Where am I?

John You're at *(name of venue)*.

Micky I can't be!

John Why?

Micky Because I'm king, that's why.

John A king? Hardly, you're our mate, Micky.

Micky You're joking. Don't say I was only dreaming!

John You were only dreaming.

Micky Oi! I said don't say I was only dreaming. Oh, what a shame. It was a wonderful dream. I – yes, I – was a great, powerful king, dressed in fine clothes and wearing a crown.

John You?

Micky I had lots of servants that I could boss around.

John I bet you enjoyed that!

Micky Servants who did my housework for me. Servants to fan me and keep me cool. Servant girls dropping grapes into my mouth. What a life!

John   Dream on!

Micky   I intend to! I had a Rolls-Royce to go shopping in, a golden shopping trolley, a bit like a chariot, and adoring crowds waving and bowing to me! No waiting in queues for me, *and* I had millions of bananas. I love being king!

John   Micky, kings do more than just boss everyone around all day.

Micky   What?

John   There's more to being a king than just wearing fine clothes, riding around in chariots and waving to your adoring crowds! It's about wanting the best for your people, making sure they have good homes and plenty to eat.

Micky   I'm still tired! I'm going to go back to sleep in my bag and enjoy being a king again. Bye!

Bible story

Matthew 21:1-11

There's a story about a king in the Bible.

The crowds were waving and cheering, but he didn't have fine clothes, or servants to boss around. He had great power and he used his power for the good of his people. He fed them and healed them.

He wasn't rich – in fact he was poor. He didn't have a horse – he had a donkey! No fine clothes and *no* crown!

But the people didn't care! They knew he was a true king; a loving, kind king, a servant king. They cheered, they sang, they waved palm branches. A wonderful king.

The King of kings. King Jesus.

Round-up

Being a rich and powerful king doesn't mean he's great. He is only great if he treats his people well. Being rich, famous or powerful doesn't make someone great. A great person is someone who is kind and cares for others.

Prayer

Lord, thank you that Jesus is a wonderful king; powerful but kind, not rich but generous; a servant king. King of kings. Amen.

It takes courage!

Aim

If we know someone is doing something wrong then there are two things we can do. We can either ignore it and let them carry on and get away with it, or we can do something about it which may take a great deal of courage!

Song

God's people

Puppet sketch

Micky   I'm really pleased that I'm the coolest guy in my class!

John   Are you?

Micky   And I'm definitely the best-looking guy!

John   Really?

Micky   I'm pleased I'm brainy but not too brainy.

John   That's a strange thing to say!

Micky   I'm so pleased that there isn't anything strange about me!

John   Nothing strange? *(Micky interrupts)*

Micky   So no one picks on me like they pick on . . . *(hesitates)*

John   Is someone being bullied?

Mick   Nice weather for the time of year.

John   Stop trying to change the subject!

Micky   Who, me?

John   If someone is being picked on then you need to do something about it!

Micky   Me? I can't, otherwise I'll get picked on too!

John   If you saw someone beating me up, would you help me or just stand and watch?

Micky   I would help you, of course, because you're my friend.

John   Good, I'm pleased to hear it!

Micky   But it's wrong to tell tales about people.

John   It's wrong to pick on people in the first place.

Micky   I'm not!

John   It's also wrong to ignore it! Go and tell the teacher.

Micky   But, but, but . . .

John   It takes courage! But you can stop this! You can make a difference! I'll come with you if you like!

Micky   Oh, yes please! Lets go. Bye!

Bible story

The calling of Moses
Exodus 3

'Go to Egypt and tell Pharaoh to let my people go!'
   'Who me?'
   God's people, the Israelites were slaves in Egypt. God decided it was time to send someone to tell Pharaoh to let his people go. So he chose Moses.
   'Who, me?'
   'Yes, you!'
   'But I'm 80 years old.'
   'I know!' said God.
   'But Pharaoh is the powerful king of a great nation.'
   'I know,' said God.
   'But I'm just a shepherd.'
   'I know,' said God.
   'I'm a runaway coward!'
   'I know!' said God
   'But, but, but . . . I'm not very good with words!'
   'I know. Look, my people are slaves, beaten and mistreated,' said God.
   'I know!' said Moses!
   'You can do something about it.'
   'I know.'
   So Moses went to the great Pharaoh and through God's power the Israelites were set free.

Round-up

There's more to being courageous than climbing high mountains or doing amazing things. You are courageous when you stand up for what is right even though others may choose to do what is wrong.

Prayer

Lord, please give us the courage to do what is right and to stand up to those who are doing wrong. Amen.

Learn to listen to learn

Aim

To show the importance of listening to what is being said, otherwise you miss out on what's going on.

Song

Speak, Lord or
One or two words

Puppet sketch

John   (*to audience*) Ralph was going shopping and he asked me if I needed anything. I hope he's remembered everything. I needed a map for a journey, some fruit jellies – yum, yum, I'll enjoy those – a white shirt – I hope he remembers my size – and a meat pie for dinner tonight! Here comes Ralph now. Ralph, did you manage to get all the shopping OK?

Ralph   Of course! (*takes out a cap*) Here you are!

John   What's this?

Ralph   It's the cap you asked for.

John   I didn't ask for a cap. I asked for a map! I thought you didn't seem to be listening, you were busy looking at the bus timetable.

Ralph   Oh, dear. Oh, well. Here are your wellies.

John   Wellies? I didn't ask for wellies. I wanted fruit jellies!

Ralph   Oh, dear. Oh, well. Here you are.

John   What's this? A skirt! I didn't want a skirt – *I wanted a shirt!*

Ralph   Oh, dear! Wrong again! I wondered why you wanted a tie to go with a skirt.

John   Tie? What tie? I wanted a pie for dinner! We can't eat tie! Oh, Ralph! What a waste of money. You really do have to listen carefully when someone gives you instructions. It's important to listen to learn.

Ralph   I'm sorry. I think I had better go. I think I've bought the wrong things for other people too!

Bible story

1 Samuel 3

There was a boy in the Bible called Samuel, who didn't live in a house, or an apartment. He lived in a huge tent. It was actually a temple called the 'Tabernacle'. He lived there with a priest called Eli.

One night they were both sleeping in their rooms when God suddenly spoke, not to Eli, the priest, but to Samuel, the boy.

Samuel didn't realise it was God speaking to him, he thought that it must be Eli. So he ran to Eli's room.

'Yes? You called me!' said Samuel.

'I didn't call you. Go back to bed,' said Eli.

'That's strange,' thought Samuel as he made his way back to his bed, 'maybe I was dreaming!'

Samuel had no sooner dropped off to sleep again when suddenly, 'Samuel!'

Samuel woke up. It was definitely Eli this time! So he bounced out of bed and ran to Eli. 'I'm coming!' he called.

'Samuel, what are you doing?' asked Eli.

'You called me,' Samuel answered.

'I didn't! Now get to bed!' replied Eli who was a bit annoyed at having been woken up twice.

Samuel went back to bed. He was very confused, but it didn't stop him sleeping and soon he fell fast asleep again.

'Samuel!' The voice came again.

Samuel jumped out of bed and once again went to Eli. 'Did you call me?' he asked.

'NO! I didn't! Now get to . . .' Eli paused. 'I didn't call you. God must be calling you. So, when God calls you again, sit up and say, "Speak, Lord, your servant is listening."'

Samuel went back to bed and sure enough the voice came again. Samuel sat up in bed and said, 'Speak, Lord, your servant is listening.' And God gave Samuel a very important message. Samuel listened very carefully because he didn't want to miss any of it. Then he went and told Eli about the message. We need to listen and learn.

Round-up

Recently, a teacher gave up teaching in England to teach in Africa where he will receive hardly any pay. When he was asked why he was giving up a good job to do this, he said, 'I've taught in Africa before and I never had to tell them to pay attention. The children long to learn and listen very carefully because they know they are the lucky ones who get an education.'

When we don't listen we get things wrong; we don't learn in the way we should and we miss out. We have two ears and only one mouth, so we should do twice as much listening as talking!

Prayer

Lord, thank you for people who can teach us so many things. I pray that we will learn to listen more. Amen.

Never turned away

Theme: Self-esteem; September or after school holidays

Aim

Often we turn our backs on people and reject them for many different reasons. We need to get rid of our prejudice and accept people for who they are.

Song

Nobody's a nobody or
Never, never, never

Puppet sketch

John *(to dog puppet)* Hey, Ralph! Did you have a nice holiday?

Ralph It was all right, I suppose.

John Only all right? You went to Blackpool, didn't you? Did you go on the rides at the fair?

Ralph I waited in a queue for one ride for almost an hour. I was just about to get on when the guy said, 'You're too small.' I was turned away!

John Poor Ralph. What did you do?

Ralph I joined a queue for a small roundabout, but they said I was too big! I was turned away again! I decided to leave the fair.

John Then what did you do?

Ralph I saw some people getting ready to pick teams for a game of football. The two captains chose their team, but neither of them chose me. They told me to get lost! I decided to go to the cinema. I joined the queue. Then I realised I didn't have enough money. So I was turned away. I went back to the caravan site and that's when I saw her!

John Saw who?

Ralph Cor! She was ace! I really fancied her! So I went up to her to chat her up!

John What did you say?

Ralph 'Hello beautiful', but she just laughed and walked off! See, everyone keeps turning me away. No one loves me!

John It's horrible when you are rejected and feel unwanted. *(to the audience)* But we love him, don't we!

Ralph *(Ralph jigs around a little)* Oh, thanks, you've made my day. You've really cheered me up. I'm off. Bye!

Bible story

Jesus heals a man with leprosy
Mark 1:40-45

Imagine that you lived at the time of Jesus, in his country. One day you were having a wash when you suddenly noticed that your skin was flaking and sore with lots of white patches. You asked someone what it was and they said that you had caught the dreaded skin disease called leprosy. In those days they believed that if someone touched something a leper had touched, that person would catch leprosy too. Since you didn't want that to happen it meant that you would have to pack your bags and leave your family, friends and home, and go to live in a lonely place. You would gradually become weaker and weaker until you died. There was no cure.

It must have been terribly lonely; no one could help you. If you walked down a street where there were people, they might throw stones at you and scream, 'leper!'

One day, a leper heard that Jesus was in a nearby town. He knew Jesus was someone great. He had heard that he had actually healed lepers! So the leper went into the town. He came to a street and there, at the other end, was Jesus surrounded by a large crowd.

He shouted as loud as he could, 'Jesus!'

Jesus and the crowd turned round.

'Err . . . a leper!' uttered the crowd, getting ready to throw stones.

'If you want to, Jesus,' continued the leper, 'you could heal me!'

'I want to,' Jesus answered. So he left the crowd and walked towards the leper. He reached out and touched him. At once the disease left him and he was clean! Jesus did not reject him, or turn him away.

Round-up

Jesus could have said, 'OK, I'll heal you, but stay where you are and don't get too close', but Jesus knew that this man had not had any human contact for a long time. That is why he not only healed him, but also touched him, showing the leper that he was accepted and special.

Prayer

Father God, help us to be like you, loving and caring. Help us never to turn anyone away. Amen.

New faces

Theme: Welcoming; new term

Aim

To help children see how important it is to accept new children and to make them feel welcome.

Song

VIP *or*
Nobody's a nobody

Puppet sketch

Micky Oh, John, there's a new boy in my class at school and he's so funny!

John Funny? You mean he tells jokes?

Micky No, he looks funny! And he talks funny! He's got huge ears!

John All the better to hear with!

Micky So I said, 'What are those satellite dishes doing sticking out of the side of your head!' Everyone laughed!

John You said what?

Micky And his legs are like tree trunks! He's a funny grey colour too and   guess what – he drinks through his nose! So I then called him 'hose nose'! We had such a laugh!

John Was the new boy laughing?

Micky No.

John I remember when you first started that school: you didn't know anyone, but you said how one person asked you to join in a game of football and made you feel really welcome. Now you enjoy going! Did you ask the new boy if he wanted to play football?

Micky No chance! He would probably crush the ball.

John So you didn't make him feel welcome at all? You should always go out of your way to make new friends. Fancy taking the micky out of an elephant.

Micky What did you say? *(he starts to shake)*

John Yes, Micky. I'd heard that a little elephant was going to be starting at your school. I thought, 'Micky will make him feel welcome,' but you didn't. Elephants soon grow and they never forget, so I think you had better apologise, don't you?

Micky I'm going, so I can plan what to say and try to make it up to him.

Bible story

Ruth 1 and 2

Many years ago, in a place called Bethlehem, there was a terrible famine. There was not enough food to feed the animals let alone the people.

So a man, his wife, Naomi, and their two sons left their home at Bethlehem in search of food. They travelled for many days until they found food in a new country.

They were all happy in their new country. The boys grew up and became lads. They both got girlfriends and then married, so the family grew in number.

Then one day Naomi's husband died. They were all very upset, but she thought, 'At least I have my two sons with their wives, Ruth and Orpah.'

But ten years later Naomi's two sons also died. Naomi was very upset. Many years before, when she had left Bethlehem, she had a husband and two sons, but now they had all died.

She said to her two daughters-in-law, 'I am going back to my home, back to Bethlehem, back to my own people. You go back to your families. You are both young. Marry again.'

They waved her goodbye and watched as she walked off into the distance.

Suddenly Ruth shouted, 'Don't make me leave you! I want to come with you!'

So Ruth joined Naomi and they headed for Bethlehem.

When they arrived, all the people were overjoyed to see Naomi again and made her feel very welcome, but Ruth was a foreigner. She wore different kinds of clothes and ate different types of food.

Ruth went to work out in the fields, but none of the other workers were very friendly. They probably talked behind her back, 'Look at her strange clothes and she does talk funny!'

But the owner of the field said to his workers, 'Make her feel welcome. Isn't it a great thing that she has done, giving up her home and family in order to help Naomi! Make sure she gets plenty of corn.'

From then on everyone made her feel welcome. She went on to marry the owner of the field and Bethlehem became her new home!

Round-up

It's great to meet new people. We can learn new things and make new friends. Let's go out of our way to welcome new people.

Prayer

Lord, help us to remember what it's like to be a newcomer, or a stranger, and I pray that we will always do our best to make people feel welcome. Amen.

New start

Theme: Beginning of the year

Aim

To show that we can all change and have a new start!

Song

VIP *or*
Think about such things

Puppet sketch

Preparation: Draw 8 simple pictures, 2 sets of 4.
Set 1
- a picture of frogspawn (two circles with a black spot in the middle)
- two tadpoles
- two tadpoles developing legs
- two frogs

Set 2
- a caterpillar
- a chrysalis
- a chrysalis beginning to open
- a butterfly

John   I've been drawing some pictures.

Micky   This should be a laugh!

John   Oi! I'll show you the pictures and I want you to guess what they are, Micky.

Micky   All right!

(John shows the picture of the frogspawn)

Micky   Two big eyes!

John   No they're not two big eyes. I'll show you the next one! *(shows the two tadpoles)*

Micky   Two lollipops!

John   No! I'll show you the third! *(shows the two tadpoles with legs)*

Micky   Two lollipops with legs?

John   They are not lollipops! I'll show you the next. *(shows the two frogs)*

Micky   Two green lollipops!

John   They are not lollipops!! I think I'll show my pictures to the children to see if they know what they are!

(John goes through the same pictures in the same order – hopefully the children will recognise the pictures.)

Isn't it amazing to think that this *(shows picture 1)* changes into this! *(shows picture 4)*

I've got some more pictures to show you, Micky. *(shows the next four pictures but once again Micky guesses incorrectly)*
- caterpillar *(Micky says it's a toothbrush with a head!)*
- chrysalis *(Micky says it's an egg)*
- chrysalis beginning to open *(Micky says, 'Oops, who broke the egg?')*
- a butterfly *(Micky says it's a flutterby)*

(Go through the pictures with the children.)

John   Isn't it amazing to think that this caterpillar changes into a beautiful butterfly. A new start! We can have a new start too!

Micky   What? Will I grow wings? Will I be able to fly?

John   No, but listen to this story.

Micky   OK, bye!

Bible story

Zacchaeus
Luke 19:1-10

There was a man in Jericho and he was rich!

People sometimes think that if you're rich you automatically have lots of friends and are always happy. But this man didn't have many friends and therefore couldn't have been very happy!

You see he had a job that was well paid but made him very unpopular. He was a tax collector! This meant that he took the people's money and gave it to the Romans!

The Romans were a strong army who had come into their country and taken over! They bossed the people around and told them what to do and demanded that they paid them money called taxes. The people who collected the money were called 'tax collectors'; they were often cheats and the people hated them!

Jesus had come to town and everyone wanted to see him.

There was a small man called Zacchaeus at the back of the crowd. He couldn't see but there was no way the crowd was going to let him through. He was a cheat. He was a traitor. He was a tax collector! Yes, a dreaded tax collector! But he longed to see Jesus so he ran off up the road and climbed up a tree. Yes, I said a tree! Can you imagine a rich man, probably wearing an expensive suit, climbing up a tree? Jesus and the crowd walked along the road and stopped right underneath the tree! Jesus looked up. The crowd looked up! There he was, a rich man sitting in the tree. The crowd probably laughed, 'Look at him, a rich man in a tree.'

Jesus said, 'Zacchaeus, come on down, I want to come to your house.'

'Wow, he knows my name and wants to come to my house!' thought Zacchaeus.

The crowd was angry. 'Jesus, don't you know who he is? He's a cheat, he's a tax collector, he is no good!' But Jesus didn't care what the people thought and went back to his house to chat! The crowd grumbled and moaned.

But after a while Zacchaeus came out and he had changed! He said to the crowd, 'If I have cheated you out of any money then I'll pay you back four times the amount!' The crowd was speechless!

No one had time for Zacchaeus but Jesus did and Zacchaeus changed! A new start.

Round-up

Although we may never turn into a frog like a tadpole, or into a butterfly like a caterpillar, we can have a new start. If we've been using our hands to destroy things, we can use them to build and do good things. If we've used our mouths to say nasty things we can use them to say good things. We can change and become better people!

Prayer

Father God, we thank you that you have time for us and never give up on us. Thank you that we can have a new start through you. Amen.

Nobody's a nobody

Theme: Respect

Aim

To show that everyone, however old or young, is important, that nobody is a nobody.

Song

Nobody's a nobody or
God's people

Puppet sketch

John   *(calling to puppet in bag)* Come on, Micky! Everyone is waiting!

Micky   Hang on, I'm just getting ready!

John   Since when have you ever bothered getting ready for an assembly? *(or church service if that is what you are taking)*

Micky   Get them to shout, 'We want Super Micky!'

John   Pardon?

Micky   You heard. Get them to shout, 'We want Super Micky!'

John   OK everyone, you heard what he said, so after three: 1 . . . 2 . . . 3 . . . We want Super Micky! *(Micky flies out of the bag like a superhero)* Micky, what are you doing?

Micky   It's not plain, ordinary Micky anymore. It's Super Micky! Faster than a speeding car, stronger than the strongest elephant, more handsome than *(latest heart-throb)*. I am here to rescue ladies in dresses!

John   You mean ladies in distress.

Micky   That's what I said!

John   What's this all in aid of, Micky?

Micky   You mean 'Super Micky'! I'm here to help people and to make a difference. To clean up the streets!

John   I'll get you a broom.

Micky   I mean, to rid the streets of crime and make this place a safer place to live in.

John   Look Micky, that's very brave of you, but we have trained police to do that. You could get hurt. These people are often violent and much stronger than you.

Micky   Yes, but it's boring being me. Just plain and ordinary!

John   You're not boring and you're definitely not plain and ordinary! We like you the way you are!

Micky: What? Really?

John   Yes, really!

Micky   Really, really, really, really?

John   Yes! Really, really, really, really!

Micky   Wow! Then I'm off to get rid of this silly cape! Bye!

Bible story

Moses
Exodus

Just imagine that you were born, not in this century or in this country, but thousands of years ago in Egypt! But, you were not an Egyptian; you were an Israelite slave. You had to work very hard for no pay and if you didn't work hard enough you would be treated cruelly and be whipped, or hit.

Some of the older slaves talked about a God who would send a deliverer who would tell Pharaoh to let God's people go; but you didn't believe them.

Then one day, there was a lot of excitement in the camp.

'He's here,' the people cried.

'Who?' you called.

'The deliverer!'

You were excited too. You had to see him. What would he be like? You imagined a mighty warrior with a chariot pulled by white horses, but all you could see was an old man! 'What, him? What can he do?'

But after a time strange things began to happen. The rivers turned to blood, then came thousands of frogs leaping around everywhere, then gnats, flies, dead animals, boils, hailstones as big as cricket balls, and thousands of locusts; then it stayed dark for many days, then came the Passover. Eventually Pharaoh not only said that all the slaves could leave, but he begged them to leave. God had worked through an 80-year-old man called Moses.

Round-up

Sometimes God used mighty people to do his work, other times he used wise people, but in this case he chose an old man of 80 to lead his people. It was a very important and demanding job! Moses thought that he was a nobody, but God didn't think so. God had been training Moses to lead his people for many years.

Prayer

Father God, thank you that nobody is a nobody. We are all unique, all with something special to offer. Amen.

One lie leads to another

Aim

To show that if you lie, or make up stories to try to get out of a situation, you will soon find that no one will trust you; and often if you lie once about something you have to lie again to cover up. It's better to tell the truth in the first place.

Song

One or two words or
Think about such things

Puppet sketch

John   Hey, Micky! I heard you were late for school yesterday.

Micky   What me? Never!

John   That's not what Tango said!

Micky   No! He's making it up!

John   That's strange, because your teacher also told me you were late.

Micky   Yes, I own up. I missed the bus.

John   How come?

Micky   Tango shouted that the bus was early and was coming down the road, but I didn't believe him.

John   Why would Tango tell you the bus was coming if it wasn't?

Micky   Nice weather!

John   What? Oh, dear! What have you been up to?

Micky   Nothing, honest!

John   I know you Micky, you have. Now what is it?

Micky   Well, I like to play Tango up a bit, so three days on the trot I shouted to him that the bus was early. I watched from the bedroom window as Tango quickly grabbed his bag and coat and ran as fast as he could down to the bus stop. It was very funny watching his little legs going so fast. But when he got to the stop, the bus was nowhere in sight! So then I coolly walked down to the stop at the right time. He was not a happy chappy.

John   What a rotten trick to play on him – and three times on the trot!

Micky   When he called that the bus was coming I thought he was getting his own back and was pulling my leg, so I didn't believe him. But he was telling the truth! So I missed the bus and got into trouble for being late!

John   Oh, dear! Well I hope you have learnt your lesson. That just goes to show that you shouldn't joke about things like that, or tell lies. It doesn't pay and it backfires. People will never know whether they can believe you, or not.

Micky   I'd better go before I miss the bus!

Bible story

Joseph is betrayed by his brothers
Genesis 37:1-36

There was a boy in the Bible called Joseph who had eleven brothers. Fancy that! Enough for a whole football team in one family. The only problem was that they didn't get on! Joseph, the second-youngest brother, was the favourite son of Jacob, their father, and was spoilt rotten. He didn't have to work as hard as they did and their father even bought him a very special coat. He loved his coat and loved to show off in it.

He had dreams about his brothers and his father. He dreamt that they were bowing down to him.

'Who does he think he is?' the brothers moaned. He always told Jacob all the things his brothers had been up to, often getting them into trouble.

Eventually Joseph's older brothers had had enough. They decided to kill him, then changed their minds and decided to sell him as a slave instead.

They lied to their father by ripping Joseph's coat and covering it in blood and pretended that a wild animal had attacked him and killed him. Jacob was heartbroken that his son had been killed in this way.

The brothers thought that they had got away with it, but they didn't realise that God was looking after Joseph.

Many years went by and there was a terrible famine. There wasn't any food anywhere, except in Egypt. So Jacob said to his remaining sons, 'You must go to Egypt and try to buy some food!'

They set off to Egypt, but they didn't realise that their brother, Joseph, had been made second-in-command in Egypt. He was now a very great and powerful man.

Imagine how Joseph felt when he saw his brothers who had sold him in to slavery all those years ago. They were now bowing down before him, just like in the dream.

Imagine how Joseph's brothers felt when they suddenly realised that they had been found out: the terrible thing they had done to Joseph, the many lies they had told their father. There was Joseph standing before them with the power to have them killed.

Joseph didn't kill them. After a lot of tears he forgave them. His father was overjoyed to see him alive again and they all went and lived with Joseph in Egypt.

(Other Bible passages on telling the truth: Proverbs 6:15, 13:5; Ephesians 4:25.)

Round-up

It is important to tell the truth. If you tell the truth then people will trust you, but if you often tell lies no one will know whether they can trust you or not! You're the one who will lose out in the end.

Prayer

Lord, help us to see how important it is to tell the truth, even when it may be easier to tell a lie. Amen.

Sharing

Theme: Christian Aid Week

Aim

To show how important it is to include everyone. It's important to look out for those who may be overlooked for whatever reason.

Song

VIP

Puppet sketch

John   Micky, how did the party at school go? *(to audience)* Micky's school put on a special party to raise money for Christian Aid. The idea was that everyone made something to eat, like cake, or a trifle. Then you would buy what you wanted to eat. The money would then be passed on to the charity Christian Aid.

Micky   The party was good, so I hear, but it made me ill.

John   Oh, dear, what do you think caused that?

Micky   Mum made me a banana trifle to take to the party.

John   I bet that was popular! When did you start feeling ill? Did you join in the games?

Micky   Er, no.

John   What about the disco?

Micky   Er, no.

John   What a shame. You love games and you have a unique style of dancing.

Micky   I thought I had better try out the trifle first, just to make sure that it was all right.

John   I see. Was it?

Micky   Oh, yes, it was yummy! That's when I spotted my friend under the table.

John   Under the table! What was he doing under there?

Micky   His mum had made a cake so he thought he had better make sure it was OK. He thought he needed a second opinion, so he asked me if I would try a slice. I was happy to oblige.

John   I bet you were!

Micky   He gave my mum's trifle a second opinion and somehow one slice led to another and before long the trifle and cake had both gone!

John   What! You two ate all the trifle and cake! No wonder you feel ill! How could you be so greedy? It was made to help raise money for Christian Aid, but you two ate it all and made yourselves sick. Serves you right! A lot of people would have enjoyed that trifle and cake. You could have made lots of money for Christian Aid, and you would have enjoyed the party far more because you would have been able to join in the games and the disco.

Micky   I never thought of that! I'm sorry. Maybe I can do something else to help.

John   Yes, off you go and try to think of something!

Micky   Bye!

Bible story

Naboth's vineyard
1 Kings 21

There was a king called Ahab in the Bible who had a huge garden. One day he was admiring his garden when he happened to look over the wall. He couldn't believe his eyes! There was a small, beautiful, but-well-looked after vineyard.

The king thought to himself, 'I want that!' So he went round to see his next-door neighbour.

'Hello,' he said as his neighbour opened the door, 'I'm the king and I want your vineyard. How much will it cost me?'

His neighbour, whose name was Naboth, replied, 'Oh, I am sorry King, but my vineyard is not for sale!'

'Oh, come on!' said the king, 'I will give you a fair price for it! So do not mess me around!'

But once again Naboth replied, 'It's not for sale. You see, it's been my family's land for generations!'

The king left and went back to the palace and sulked, and sulked, muttering to himself, 'It's not fair.'

The queen, whose name was Jezebel and who was a very wicked

lady, saw him and said, 'Why are you sulking?'

'I'm not,' replied the king.

'Yes, you are. Now tell me!' she shouted.

'Well, you know our neighbour, Naboth. He has a vineyard and I want it, so I offered to buy it from him, but he said no! It's not fair!'

Queen Jezebel laughed at him, 'You are the king, aren't you? You can have whatever you want! I'll get it for you!'

So off she went. She told some wicked lies against Naboth and had him arrested and put to death!

'Oh, husband dear,' she said to the king, 'Naboth is no more and the vineyard is yours!

The king was so happy, he danced for joy, but God was very angry. You see he hates it when big people pick on little people. He hates it when rich people aren't fair to poor people.

He said to the king and queen, 'Because you have done such a wicked thing, I will get rid of you in the same way you got rid of my servant, Naboth.'

And that's exactly what happened.

Round-up

You see, the king had a huge garden so he didn't need Naboth's small vineyard, but because he was so greedy he took it away from Naboth.

Prayer

Lord, we thank you for the different things we have. Help us not to be greedy, constantly wanting more, but help us to be generous and share what we have. Amen.

Stick together

Theme: Team work

Aim

To show the importance of team work, sticking together, valuing each other, being committed and never giving up!

Song

Nobody's a nobody or
Anytime, anywhere

Puppet sketch

John Hey Micky, I was really proud of you on Saturday.

Micky Thank you very much.

John *(to audience)* Micky and his team entered an 'It's a Knockout' competition. That's when different teams compete against each other in crazy races and competitions.

Micky Our team won! That's why John is proud of us.

John I'm not proud of you because you won!

Micky Why then? Is it because I was the best-looking guy there?

John Were you? No, that's not the reason!

Micky Is it because I did all those races but still didn't have a hair out of place!

John No!

Micky Why then?

John There was a guy there called Tango and no one else wanted him in their team but you did!

Micky Yes, Tango is an orang-utan. He has long hair and long arms which means he's not very good at running because he trips over his hair and arms, and he is very clumsy.

John But you wanted him in your team and what a team member he was!

Micky   You can say that again! He's not very good at running but he's so strong. So we won the tug-of-war no problem. In fact we won every game that involved strength.

John   That's one reason I was proud of you. No one else wanted Tango but you did! The other reason for being proud of you was that all the other teams were shouting and blaming each other when things went wrong. But your team didn't do that, you did the opposite: you encouraged one another and just had fun! And that's more important than winning! That's what makes a really good team!

Micky   I think you're right. Hey, guess what! Tango and I are best friends now!

John   Great, I'm pleased to hear it!

Bible story

Paralysed man
Luke 5:17-26; Matthew 9:1-8; Mark 2:1-12

There were four friends who had a friend who was paralysed. Every day they would carry their friend out and put him on the side of the street. People would see the man and feel sorry for him and give him some money. But this particular day they picked him up on his mat as usual, but they didn't put him down on the side of the street – they kept going. 'Er, excuse me, you forgot to put me down,' said the paralysed man.

'No, we haven't,' the others said, 'we're taking you to see Jesus.'

They were probably very hot because they lived in a hot country! But they didn't give up!

They would have had aching arms and legs and sore hands! But they didn't give up!

Jesus was in a house and there was a huge crowd of people all around. But they didn't give up!

They went round the side of the house and there were some steep, narrow steps to the roof. It would have been difficult to carry him up! But they didn't give up!

Now, they had to make a hole in the roof. But they didn't give up.

The bits fell on the people below. But they didn't give up.

They had to find a way of lowering their friend down to Jesus! But they didn't give up!

Jesus looked up at the friends on the roof and was amazed by their faith!

He looked at the man on the mat and said, 'Your sins are forgiven.'

'Only God is allowed to forgive sins,' thought the crowd.

Jesus said, 'Which is the easier to say? "Your sins are forgiven," or "Get up, take up your bed and walk"? To prove the Son of man has authority to forgive sins on earth.' – he spoke to the paralysed man – 'Get up, take your bed and walk!'

And he did!

Everyone was so excited, especially the four friends on the roof who never gave up and brought their friend to Jesus!

Round-up

Let's stick together even when the going gets tough. We need each other. Together we are strong.

Prayer

Lord, I thank you that we are all different. We are all unique with something special to offer! Help us to value one another and work together as a team. Amen.

There's no place like home

Theme: Homelessness; winter

Aim

To show that we all need a shelter. We all need a place we call 'home'. To point out that there are many people who have no home, or real shelter, and that everything that can be done to help them needs to be done.

Song

Never, never, never *or*
Give me your love, Lord

Puppet sketch

Micky   My friend played a terrible trick on me.

John   What was that?

Micky   I washed my hat and hung it on the line to dry. Suddenly it started to rain. So I dashed outside to get it in. But my friend locked the door, so I got soaked through!

John   I got soaked once. I was out walking. It was a lovely summer's day and I was wearing a T-shirt and shorts. Suddenly a big grey cloud blocked out the sun, the wind started to blow and down came the rain, which then turned to hail. I ran as fast as I could, but by the time I found a place to shelter I was soaked through to the bone!

Micky   Ha-ha! That's very funny!

John   It wasn't meant to be!

Micky   The best bit about getting cold and wet is snuggling up by a nice, warm fire or heater to get warm and dry again!

John   We all need shelter. I'm going to ask the children a question. What animal protects and shelters its babies in a pouch? Yes, a kangaroo!

Micky   Must be snug, warm and safe in there!

John   We all need protection and shelter, but there are many people all over the world, even in this country, who have no shelter at all! They have no home to go to. You imagine having nowhere to go during a cold winter when there's frost and bitter cold winds.

Micky   It makes me feel cold just thinking about it. I'm going to snuggle up in my bag! Bye!

Bible story

David and the cave of Adullam
1 Samuel 22

There was a man in the Bible who found himself homeless. It was David! He had to hide from the king because the king was jealous of him.

David had become a folk hero. There had been a giant called Goliath who threatened their country. Everyone, including the king, was frightened to fight him, apart from David.

David took the giant on in a battle and beat him! The king was really pleased at first, but when he realised that the people loved David more than him, he became jealous and tried to kill David.

David found a huge cave to hide in. He told his father and brothers where it was and they came and lived in it too. David knew that the king was wrong. David needed an army and people started to join him in the cave.

But they were not brave, strong people. Some of them were weak, some were lazy and others were cowards. Some were oppressed people, runaway slaves with nowhere to go. But David didn't turn any of them away. He knew they all needed shelter and protection. David fed them, trained them and turned them into a brave army of 400. He never turned any of them away and they won many battles.

Round-up

There is a Christian charity called 'Shelter' which helps people who are homeless. Everyone should have a place of shelter.

Prayer

Lord, thank you for our homes. But, Lord, help us to remember those who have no home, who live on the streets. Thank you for charities like 'Shelter' who help the homeless. Amen.

Those who look after us

Theme: Mother's Day

Aim

To help children appreciate those who look after them and not to take them for granted.

Song

VIP or
Think about such things

Puppet sketch

John   Ralph, how's your mum?

Ralph   A bit rough.

John   Oh, dear! It's a good job she has you to help her with different things.

Ralph   Yes, I would love to help, but I'm a bit busy at the moment *(he works on something in his bag, but refuses to let anyone see).*

John   If you are too busy to help your mum when she is feeling rough, then you *are* too busy!

Ralph   Yes, I know, but this is very important!

John   Who's done the washing up?

Ralph   No one yet. Mum will probably do it later. Now stop disturbing me!

John   What about the tidying up?

Ralph   Look, can't you see how busy I am? Mum normally does it.

John   But you said that she is feeling rough. She would probably appreciate a hand with things.

Ralph   Lend her one, then!

John   I will, but she's not my mum!

Ralph   Yes, I know. I'll help later!

John   I'm shocked.

Ralph   I've finished! Look, do you think she will like it? *(Ralph shows a Mother's Day card he has just made)* It's for my mum!

John   Yes, it's very good. Can I read what it says inside?

Ralph   Yes, I think it's rather touching.

John   *(reads the card)* 'To the best mum. I promise I will help more from now on! Love from your son, Ralph.' Great! You can start by doing the washing-up.

Ralph   Later! I'm busy now. I've recorded a TV programme that I need to watch!

John   Ralph, don't say something if you don't mean it! In your card you promised to help more from now on!

Ralph   Yes, well, I haven't given her the card yet so she doesn't know what I've written.

John   Go on! Go and help her. Prove you mean what you have written. The video can wait!

Ralph   I know. You're right. I'd better go. Bye!

Bible story

Peter's mother-in-law
Mark 1:29-30

We do need to be considerate to others. For example, if the person who looks after you is feeling poorly, don't invite all your friends round and make more work for them. They will need peace and quiet!

Simon Peter in the Bible made that mistake. He was with Jesus and the disciples. Thirteen in all, and maybe one or two more, and he invited them all round to his house.

His mother-in-law was in bed with fever, so his wife was probably very worried and very busy looking after her!

The last thing she needed was for her husband to turn up with twelve of his mates. In that country it was custom to wash guests' feet and to offer them a drink and some food. That meant more work that she could well do without. So who could blame her if she was very angry with him!

But strangely enough she wasn't! You see, Jesus was with him. Jesus always helped out and had time for people. He went to see Simon Peter's mother-in-law, helped her up and at once the fever left her. She was able to join in with the others. She probably noticed that Simon

Peter was not looking after his guests very well because straight away she started to wait on them!

Round-up

Those who look after us give up so many things, like time, money, space in the house, etc. Never take them for granted. Help out where you can and thank them for all the things they do for you!

Prayer

Lord, thank you for those who look after us, for their love and generosity. Help us never to take them for granted. Amen.

What a day

Theme: Easter

Aim

To show why Easter is so special to Christians. A sad time, a confusing message, yet a time of rejoicing and celebration.

Song

On Good Friday *or*
For God so loved the world

Puppet sketch

John   *(to Micky)* I hear you had quite a day yesterday.

Micky   You can say that again! I was so excited that I woke up really early and dashed into Mum and Dad's room. But they told me to go back to bed. Had they forgotten?

John   Forgotten what?

Micky   Don't you start! Later, I went downstairs to collect my post, but there was none for me. Had everyone forgotten?

John   Forgotten what?

Micky   There were no cards, no smiling faces, and worst of all, no presents! I thought they loved me! I almost cried! Had they forgotten?

John   Forgotten what?

Micky   Then we went to Grandma's! I went inside the house when . . .

John   Surprise! *(both look happy)*

Micky   Exactly! Balloons, streamers, cheering, presents! All my family and friends!

John   Yep! A surprise birthday party.

Micky   They hadn't forgotten after all. I was so happy I almost cried.

John   Gosh, twice in one day.

Micky Yep, I had been really sad, then I was really happy! What a day! I must go, more presents to open!

Bible story

John 20

I wonder if you've been really upset, confused and overjoyed all in the same day.

It must have been like that for Jesus' friends. They had seen him taken, beaten and put to death. They were deeply upset and wept! They were scared, probably hiding in a house behind closed doors.

Suddenly there was a loud knocking at the door! 'Who's there?' they asked.

'Mary!' came the reply. 'He's gone!'

'Who's gone?' they asked.

'Him!'

'Him who?'

'Jesus!' Mary told them.

'We know,' said the friends, 'we saw him die!'

'I went to the tomb, but his body has gone!' wept Mary.

Peter and John raced to the tomb. It was true. Jesus' body had gone like Mary had said! His grave clothes were there, but Jesus' body was gone! The two of them were very upset and confused as they explained to the others that it was true, Jesus' body had gone.

Suddenly Jesus was standing there. He was alive again! He spoke to them and ate with them. They were amazed, scared, confused, excited and overjoyed all at the same time.

What a day. Jesus was alive again!

Round-up

This is why Easter is such a special time for Christians. A time to remember why Jesus died and to celebrate because he is alive again.

Prayer

Lord, thank you for this wonderful story. Help us to understand what Easter is really all about. Amen.

Who's the greatest?

Aim

People often look up to pop stars, TV stars, or sports people. They think that famous people are great people. The Bible says great people are people who serve others (Mark 10:43).

Song

Image of God or
VIP

Puppet sketch

Micky   Two new boys joined our class today. They are brothers, Gary and Gordon Bennett. In fact they are twins, almost identical.

John   What are they like?

Micky   Gary appears to be a real cool dude; tells great jokes, a fast runner and excellent at football. All the girls think he's cute!

John   What about Gordon Bennett?

Micky   He was a little shy today and his jokes weren't funny. He came last in a running race we had and he is absolutely useless at football!

John   Seeing as they are almost identical twins, do the girls think Gordon is cute as well?

Micky   No! They think Gary is much better looking! In fact within one day Gary has become the most popular person in school! They all think he's great! But I don't!

John   Micky, you're not jealous because he's so popular, are you?

Micky   No! But he did pinch my chair during dinner. I got up for a second and when I came back he was sitting in my chair!

John   Oh, dear!

Micky   During a game of football, he was on the other team. He got the ball and dribbled round our team, but I managed to tackle him fair and square. He didn't like that and when no one was looking he tripped me up, kicked me really hard and laughed at me!

John   Oh, dear!

Micky   No one else noticed, but then he came at me with the ball again. I got ready to tackle him when suddenly he pushed me. I went flying! He laughed and then everyone joined in! Then they carried on with the game, leaving me on the ground with a cut knee.

John   What? No one helped you?

Micky   Yes, Gordon did. He helped me get up and took me to the first-aid teacher, to get a plaster.

John   What, Gordon? Gary's twin?

Micky   Yes. He's a great guy. Anyone who will stop playing football to help someone else is pretty great, I reckon. A mate you can rely on!

John   What about Gary?

Micky   He's not as great as he thinks he is. It's a shame he's not more like Gordon. Bye!

Bible story

Jesus washes his disciples' feet
John 13:1-10

The country where Jesus lived is a really hot country. People had to walk for miles along dusty tracks. This meant that their feet soon became dirty, sweaty and very smelly. The custom was that if you were a guest in someone's home, your feet would be washed, normally by one of the least-important servants. What a horrible job, especially if there were large numbers of guests.

One day, Jesus and his friends hired an upper room for a meal, but of course this meant that there was no servant to wash their feet. I can imagine some of the older disciples trying to persuade one of the younger ones to go round and wash everyone's feet. Of course no one would want to volunteer to wash thirteen pairs of dirty, smelly feet!

Suddenly Jesus got up, took off his outer garment, tied a towel around his waist and started to wash his friends' feet. They were really embarrassed! Jesus was their leader. He was a really important man, a great teacher. He could perform fantastic miracles like walking on the water and making blind people see! He was the greatest person any of them had ever met and yet here he was, washing their dirty, smelly feet!

Simon Peter couldn't keep quiet. 'You are not going to wash my feet! Never!' he said.

Jesus said, 'If I do not wash your feet you will no longer be my disciple.'

'Oh, wash my hands and my head, too!' answered Peter.

'If you have had a bath, you are completely clean, except for your feet!' replied Jesus.

Peter was amazed that such a great man as Jesus was prepared to do such a horrible job, but by being prepared to become like a servant Jesus showed that he was a truly great man.

Round-up

One day you may write a book, or a play, or become a famous singer or sports person, and people may say that you are really great. But remember, truly great people are those who go out of their way to serve and help others.

Prayer

Lord, thank you that we don't have to be famous to be great, but that we need to be prepared to help others in whatever way we can. Amen.

You're amazing!

Theme: Look after yourself

Aim

To show that our bodies are like a machine – very carefully designed, every organ having an important part to play. We need to look after it.

Song

Image of God or
Cartoon land

Puppet sketch

John   Micky, do you look after yourself?

Micky   What do you mean?

John   Well, your body is fantastic. Do you look after it?

Micky   Thank you very much! Of course I look after it. I'm a healthy dude!

John   Good. How?

Micky   I comb my hair . . .

John   Really?

Micky   Cheek! I clean my teeth, cut my nails and even have a bath!

John   Cor! I am impressed! But looking after yourself means more than just looking like a cool dude on the outside. It means looking after your insides too.

Micky   Yuck! How do you do that? You can't take your insides out and give them a wash, can you?

John   It means being careful about what you eat!

Micky   I like bananas!

John   Good. They are very good for you.

Micky   Bananas and chips!

John   Yuck! Chips are OK occasionally, but not all the time. You need a balanced diet. What about sleep? Do you get plenty of rest?

Micky It depends on the lesson I'm in at school. If it's a bit boring then I get plenty of sleep.

John No, seriously, Micky. Someone your age needs nine to twelve hours sleep each night, otherwise you become tired and grumpy.

Micky My mate smokes because he says that it makes him look cool. Is that bad for you?

John Does it make him look cool?

Micky No! He looks a bit like a chimney and he smells like one too!

John People who smoke are pumping themselves full of dirty pollution. The body is not designed to take it, so it makes people cough and they are choked up. They're spending lots of money just to make themselves ill . . . What about exercise?

Micky I run for the bus every morning!

John Micky, we only have one body and it's got to last us for the rest of our lives, anything up to a hundred years! So we need to look after it. That means a balanced diet, exercise, enough rest and keeping away from things that are no good for us. Remember you're amazing, so keep it that way!

Micky Cor! I'm amazing! I think it's time for me to go and get some rest! Bye!

Bible story

Psalm 139
This is what the Psalmist said to God.
'You created every part of me. You put me together in my mother's womb.'
We have been carefully put together, carefully designed. You are very precious! Look after yourself!

Round-up

If a friend gave you something to look after and said, 'This is very precious, it's worth £100,000,' you would be so careful with it.

 God has given us our bodies. We are worth far more than that, so we need to look after them.

Prayer

Lord, thank you for our bodies. Thank-you that every member has an important part to play. Help us to be sensible and to look after ourselves carefully. Amen.

Resources

Music

All the songs mentioned in this book appear in *34 Songs for All Occasions*, a music book and CD by John Hardwick.
John Hardwick: 12 Normanton Way, Histon, Cambridge, CB4 9XS.
Tel: 01223 519489
Email: johnhardwick36@hotmail.com (For website details please see Counties website.)

Kidsource – super songs for church and school by Kevin Mayhew Ltd, Buxhall, Stowmarket, Suffolk, IP14 3BW. Tel: 01449 737978
Fax: 01449 737834 Email: info@kevinmayhewltd.com

Puppet suppliers

Children Worldwide – a full range of puppets and other children's resources.

Children Worldwide, Dalesdown, Honeybridge Lane, Dial Post, Horsham, West Sussex, RH13 8NX. Tel: 01403 711032 Fax: 710716
Email: cwide@talk21.com

One Way UK – a full range of puppets and other children's resources.
One Way UK, c/o Tyndale Baptist Church, 2-4 Cressingham Road, Reading, RG2 7JE. Tel: 07071 226065 Fax: 0118 9756303
Email: info@onewayuk.com

Organisations

Children Worldwide: Has 40 Christian children's workers in the UK.
Tel: 01403 710712 Email: cwide@talk21.com
Website: www.childrenworldwide.co.uk

Scripture Union: Has over 40 Christian evangelists and schools workers in the UK. Tel: 01908 856000 Email: info@scriptureunion.org.uk
Website: www.scripture.org.uk

Counties: Has over 40 Christian evangelists, many working in schools in the UK. Tel: 01373 823013 Fax: 01373 859199
Email: counties30@aol.com
Website: http://members.aol.com/counties30

Operation Mobilisation: 'Kids and Things' children's puppet team.
Tel: 0121 585 5662 Email: julianwolton@luke.om.org